STABLE
Stereotypes

Equestrian Eccentrics

FROM **HORSE&HOUND**

KENILWORTH PRESS

Copyright © 2010 IPC Media Ltd

First published in the UK in 2010
by Kenilworth Press, an imprint of Quiller Publishing Ltd

British Library Cataloguing-in-Publication Data
A catalogue record for this book
is available from the British Library

ISBN 978 1 905693 33 7

The right of IPC Media Ltd to be identified as the author of this work has been
asserted in accordance with the Copyright, Design and Patent Act 1988

Printed in China
Book and cover design by Sharyn Troughton

Illustrations by Dianne Breeze

Kenilworth Press
An imprint of Quiller Publishing Ltd
Wykey House, Wykey, Shrewsbury, SY4 1JA
Tel: 01939 261616 Fax: 01939 261606
E-mail: info@quillerbooks.com
Website: www.kenilworthpress.co.uk

Foreword

WHEN I had the idea for a series of 'Stable Stereotypes' – an equestrian twist on the *Sunday Telegraph's* much-loved Social Stereotypes cartoons – a few years ago, I little imagined how popular they would become.

That they have testifies to the accuracy with which we captured (and occasionally tortured) assorted equestrian eccentrics. Most of us (too many of us, perhaps) know people frighteningly similar to these caricatures; the power-crazed fence judge; the suave man at the gate; the farrier who forever grumbles about his lot – then takes far smarter holidays than his clients; the well-meaning enthusiast who spends the annual GDP of Luxembourg getting nowhere on an animal worth barely £1,500…

Following the edict, 'Don't get mad – get typing' many *H&H* colleagues, myself included, have taken a turn at writing Stable Stereotypes. Often we found it a pleasantly cathartic experience amid the whirlwind of news writing, report editing and press deadlines.

Many of the resulting sketches still make me laugh out loud. And though lingering on the loo has – in my experience – always been a male habit, I hope horse lovers of every age and gender will find time somewhere between skipping out and evening stables to dip into these wonderful cameos. And then say an inward prayer that you might never become one.

Lucy Higginson
Editor
Horse & Hound

The Horse Trials Supporter

JOSEPHINE hasn't missed a British four-star three-day event in 17 years. She loves eventing. It has it all; elegance, excitement and William Fox-Pitt.

Years of experience have taught her that the best way to guarantee a front-row seat at the trot-up is to take your caravan. She shares hers with fellow aficionado Barbara, and it is strewn with programmes and members' badges from yesteryear.

She and Barbara run a private sweepstake to decide who'll be in the top three at each event, the loser buying the winner an ice-cream after the show jumping.

Josephine knows all the tricks of horse trial enjoyment, including the merits of a small thermos and a spare loo roll on cross-country day.

She has barely calmed down from the excitement of WEG – she went on a special supporters' trip – and would like to go to the big overseas events, if she could only feel at ease about the food…

The Mother from Hell

JANE has Virginia's summer programme all mapped out: the workers at Royal Windsor, the Royal, then she'll switch to doing JRNs... In fact, Jane's got Virginia's whole career mapped out, right up to the point she should have her first ride on the British young rider team. Now comes execution. Why that damn headmistress keeps phoning to request a meeting, Jane doesn't know. Haven't they seen a child with outstanding sporting ability before? She can't be expected to get to school every week.

Virginia's talent is plain to see, and she loves life on the competition circuit. The lorry is her second home (it's bigger than her first one, after all) and Jane is proud of the hours Virginia spends on the luton, discussing ringcraft and jumping technique with that nice show jumping boy she's befriended. So dedicated.

Admittedly, John doesn't get many family suppers during the show season. But his firm has an excellent canteen, and when you've got a child this talented, you have to make a few sacrifices.

The Buyer's 'Friend'

KATH is a ver', ver' experienced horsewoman. She's ridden an advanced medium dressage test (once – she scored 52%) and has been round Badminton (on a course-walk).

As such, when a friend of a friend asked her for help in finding 'the perfect schoolmaster', she immediately agreed. It's her duty to share her expertise with the wider equestrian community, and at £20 petrol money and a free lunch after each viewing, she considers herself great value.

Videoing Emma perching, petrified, on a horse that's more 'unmastered' than schoolmaster, Kath bellows: 'Sit up, shorten your reins!' If only Kath could get on and show her how it was done – what a pity she didn't bring boots and a hat.

'Don't worry,' she says, patting a shaking Emma on the shoulder as they head back to their car. 'The right horse is bound to come along soon.' But not too soon, she hopes.

The Pony Club Thruster

KATIE'S been riding since she was a zygote and was a regular on the hunting field by the age of two. Aged five, she was off the lead-rein because her mother couldn't keep up. And that's not because her mother lacks a greyhound's physique – Linford Christie would have struggled in their wake.

Katie's pony, Rocket, is a hot little chestnut whose prowess in the Prince Philip Cup proves equally useful for dodging 'oldies' in the hunting field, and opening gates at a gallop for the slow coaches, while simultaneously leaping the adjoining hedge.

Rocket weaves in and out of the other obstacles (riders), so Katie never loses sight of the huntsman – although more often than not they leave the field master in their wake.

Irritating as the precocious little mite is, she's never sent home – with the style of AP McCoy and stickability of Andrew Nicholson, she's rather handy for giving the rest of the field a lead.

The Point-to-Point Virgin

IT'S the morning of Harry's long-awaited pointing debut. It's funny, he muses, how swiftly his enthusiasm is disappearing – almost as fast as last night's Bacardi Breezers, when he was still excited (rather than terrified) about his first ever point-to-point ride.

Describing his mount, Trynottohitem, as 'regularly and fairly hunted' might have been pushing it a bit, but there's no doubt the horse has more experience than its rider. Heading to the start, Harry is now a fetching shade of green that tones well with his ill-fitting silks, jods and boots, borrowed from friends of various shapes and sizes.

When he checked Try's form in Mackenzie & Selby, Harry's

confidence was far from boosted by the comment 'Couldn't win if it started yesterday'. He just hopes to get round. Waiting at the start, he modifies this to praying not to get buried at the first fence. But then they're off, and with adrenalin coursing through his veins, he throws caution to the wind and gives it his best shot…

The Olympia Groupie

CHRISTMAS comes 10 days early for Camilla – her heart fills with the spirit of Olympia, not Bethlehem. During the annual pilgrimage on the District Line, her excitement is uncontainable, driving the entire family crackers.

Aged 10-and-three quarters, Camilla is keen to shrug off her parents anyway, and, once there, disappears on a shopping-and-autograph-hunting spree with bestest friend ever Sophie. Fortunately, since the girls consider white jodhpurs (in case someone offers them a shot on Locarno) and dayglo pink sweatshirts de rigueur Olympia garb, Mum and Dad can track them at a safe distance through the packed shopping hall.

Within an hour, six months' pocket money has gone on a programme, chips, cola, sweets, an embroidered saddlecloth (pink) for her pony, Nipper. Then it's show time. If she doesn't get Ellen Whitaker's autograph this year, Camilla will simply die. And she's almost out of space in her autograph book, having repeatedly practised signing 'Mrs Camilla Gredley' over most of the pages.

Yard Know it All

AT Happy Acres Livery, where client and staff turnover is higher than the sprawling muckheap, only one constant remains. Di has been there for years — although the boundaries between her roles of sometime client, sometime groom and self-appointed yard expert have blurred over time.

Di is, of course, the only one who really knows how to run the place. Yard managers have come and gone (some faster than others), but Di and her solid Cleveland Bay, Archie, have remained.

While Tandy, the new manager, is worried about the growing number of empty boxes, she still defers to Di when it comes to vetting potential clients. She did wonder though about Di's verdict on that thin, nervous woman with the cossetted Arabs ('I hear she beats up her horses').

Some of the other liveries don't appreciate how efficiently Di polices the arena diary, hay barn and shavings shed. But she sleeps well, confident that she's saving the owners a fortune, and basks in the respect her fellow liveries clearly have for her, testified by the silence that descends whenever she enters the tackroom.

Dianne Breeze 2006.

Point-to-Point Addict

CYNTHIA doesn't need a SatNav. Her Landy pretty much navigates the roads between Britain's point-to-point courses on its own. From January to June, her life shadows that of Julian Pritchard and Rachael Green – or so Cynthia thinks of it.

She knows all the best vantage points, parking spots, mulled wine stands and chattiest trainers in the sport.

Her wardrobe is so weatherproof, no one's quite sure if her joke about 'Gore-Tex undies' is entirely frivolous, and her tailgate picnics (once put together in the record time of 7.25min) are a pilgrimage site for the great, good (and hungry) of the pointing fraternity.

Cynthia wouldn't dream of setting off in her ancient 4x4 without the company of Curre and Llangibby, her trusty dogs. She knows the three of them go out looking a bit like lagged boilers, but she doesn't care – especially when, overlooking her sartorial shortcomings but in honour of her longevity on the ropes, her local hunt invites her to judge the best turned out.

Four-in-Hand Driver

WITH the body of Kate Moss, the arms of Arnold Schwarzenegger and the grip of a freestyle mountain climber, the four-in-hand driver has a reputation for longevity. Once proven at top level, this breed can compete until the age of 150.

With four hyped-up warmbloods and a web of reins to contend with, four-in-hand driver always has right of way at any junction near his Yorkshire yard, and many a cyclist has thrown himself into a hedge as the pounding limbs of four identikit Gelderlanders thunder towards him.

Much like an ageing shot, four-in-hand driver's hearing has been dulled by years of steel grating on tarmac, and an adjacent navigator yelling: 'left, right, up, down, STOP!' through driving obstacles around Europe. So the mid-event drinks parties he hosts from his pantechnicon are noisy affairs. But his enthusiasm as a whip is undiminished: 'If the Duke of Ed can compete in his 80s, so can I, by God!'

The Over Horsed Amateur

HAVING worked her way unsuccessfully through a string of dressage horses 'with potential' (£25,000 a pop), Lucille has decided that a grand prix schoolmaster is the way forward. Secure in the knowledge that her husband will merrily throw money at his wife's 'little hobby', Lucille calls her 'contact' in Holland. Fortunately, Hilde knows of a former Olympic short-listee who will be ideal.

Rambo, 17hh of snorting, strapping Dutch Warmblood, may once have scored 72% at grand prix, but that's not helping Lucille get more than 52% at elementary. Despite sticky breeches – and the deepest-seated saddle money can buy – little Rammie's

'elevation' practically launches Lucille into space, and her inability to find the stop-button means their schooling sessions last for several hours (until he gets bored).

Frustratingly, Lucille senses her trainer, jealous of her acquisition, is trying to curtail progress, too: 'Once you can ride a 10m circle Lucille, then we can start on pirouettes.'

The Involuntary Volunteer

JUDY Smith had no idea she'd been volunteered to run the Little Wapping Area showjumping until pony parents started pestering her for class times.

'That's what happens when you miss committee meetings,' was the chairman's coy retort. Suddenly, Judy finds she is expected to talk speeds, strides and pole lengths with the confidence of David Broome.

More alarmingly, it seems this little Pony Club show will cost about £5,000. She's tackled the local prep school, town butcher, accountants, saddlers, garage, landscape gardeners and nursery for sponsorship. She now has to paint 12 fences with company logos and repeat the names plus a 'brief' synopsis of each trade over the loudspeaker every 20 minutes – all for a grand total of £85.90.

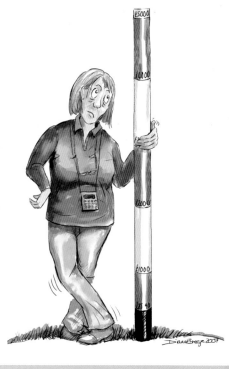

Her old life – in derivatives – was nothing compared to this.

'If I can't raise money for portaloos, they'll just have to pee in the woods,' she wails at the next committee meeting.

Someone's husband eventually coughs up. Nonetheless, Judy's praying that a freak July snowstorm might cause the whole thing to be called off.

The High Goaler's Girl

IGNACIO flies Gabby and Eduardo to England only once the thermometer touches 90°F. Even if she does look great in Armani jeans and cashmere crewnecks, the only way a high-goal wife can safely survive a polo season unmaimed by smitten Brits is to picnic and party with other Argentine ex-pats at the side of the pitch.

Eduardo has his own tiny mallet, which he doesn't relinquish until the end of July, along with his Ralph Lauren wardrobe (clearly made with him in mind, with all those polo pony motifs). Gabby claims to be tired of being told she looks just like her namesake on *Desperate Housewives*. But she loves the English polo party circuit, especially when Ignacio's new Australian patron offers them the loan of his English country house whenever they want.

The Equestrian PR

WITH a sociology degree from Bristol in the bag, Serena was made up to land a job in equestrian PR, since (as she said in her covering letter): 'This role combines my twin passions of equestrianism and above-the-line blue sky marketing strategy.'

Her parents haven't a clue what she does all day, but she's living with nice friends in Putney, and stepping out with a Wiltshire boy who shoots, so all seems well.

Suffice to say, Serena has discovered an enthusiasm for joint supplements and fly spray you would not have dreamt possible, and developed skin as thick as a rhino's.

'Just calling to see if you're able to use our press release in your mag this month,' she chirrups about 25 times a day – fuelled by skinny lattes – to increasingly short shrift from journalists.

Still, she gets to go to major shows, and has two tons of goodies to hand out to promising young riders on behalf of her clients. In her book, it beats a traineeship with Goldman Sachs any day.

Pony Club Granny

'GANGY' as granny is affectionately known, has a voice like an exhaust pipe and the complexion of a sultana.

Perpetually clad in a fawn Husky jacket, tartan slacks and sensible brown shoes, Gangy's long, skinny legs still cut it in a pair of trousers. She simply cannot tolerate the current vogue for flabby thighs among the young, and voices her contempt for every passing wobble of jodhpured cellulite – loudly.

It's a Pony Club one-day event, little Rowena is about to show jump, and Gangy has gone AWOL (she does this often). Just before Rowena's starting bell rings, Gangy's feet are found sticking out from underneath the lorry ramp.

'I needed a smoke and I needed some shade,' she rasps – though everyone knows she's hiding her 60-a-day habit from her bossy daughter.

Little Rowena duly jumps clear on a mare bred by Gangy, who has another fag to celebrate. That night, Gangy oversees the delivery of the 50th home-bred foal, then gets up at 5am as usual and scours the *Racing Post* over a mug of cheap instant coffee.

Dianne Breeze

Sally Safety

SALLY treats high-visibility like an Olympic discipline. Sure, the Funnells and Fox-Pitts may inspire young riders to take the reins – but Sally's role is to inspire the next generation to embrace dayglo. A computer analyst by day (and special constable at weekends), Sally has to fit riding around a hectic life, and her car is littered with all the accoutrements of early morning hacking. With light-reflecting brushing boots, tabards, hatbands, browbands, exercise sheets, knee pads, a jumping stick, mobile phone sleeve and bra straps (for summer), Sally's hi-vis habit is bordering on a fetish.

Tempted though she is to try hunting one year, the thought of leaving every hi-vis strip and bib behind makes Sally feel uneasy, so instead she concentrates her extra-curricular activities on training local Pony Club branches for the riding and road safety test during camp season. This year, it coincides with her 40th birthday – and little does she know that a vivid pink and yellow cake is already on order.

The Eventer-Turned Dressage Horse

PRIMA Donna always knew she was destined for glory – on her terms. A stunning black Thoroughbred/Trakehner with a beautiful bascule, she won four intros on the bounce and the Burghley Young Event Horse final.

But Donna is a hydrophobic ditch-wimp. How she condescended to negotiate the puddle of a water jump at the scene of her last win is a mystery. It was only the prospect of the lap of honour, the garlands, the pretty rosettes and the adulation at prize-giving that bribed her into even leaving the startbox. In truth, she racked up 20 pen at said water, but her single-figure dressage score secured first place regardless.

After one almighty strop at a pre-novice ditch, Donna was immediately reassigned to the dressage arena, where she is blissfully happy. She gets to wear white booties and have her hair plaited with striking white bands. And her saddle is cut away, so fetchingly, to reveal her Amazonian shoulders. Her new rider is elegant in top hat and tails – none of that unbecoming back-protector malarkey. Donna knows she looks a picture.

She piaffes from airbrushed stable to vacuumed horsebox to tooth-combed arena, without so much as a speck of ghastly mud to unnerve her delicate constitution. And as for that puffing one had to do as an eventer – so unseemly.

The Coloured Fanatic

IT is a truth universally acknowledged that when a coloured horse rolls, the **** only gets on the white bits. Dora doesn't mind, though – time spent scrubbing Double Mocha Cappuccino's patches into Persil-white submission is well spent in her book.

Since the age of eight, when her first pony was a perfect piebald, Dora has never strayed from her devotion to all things black and white. Bays, chestnuts, duns and greys are all ruled out for being terribly monotonous. Her coloured addiction now extends to other areas of her life – her entire wardrobe and accessories are fashionably two-tone, and even her hair is a strange mix of salt and pepper of which Richard Gere would be proud.

Seeing 'Cappy' through skewbald-tinted glasses, she fails to notice he has more feathers than your average aviary and enough mane to stuff a mattress. Nor, in her search for that perfect blend of brown and white patches, did she spot the nose more Roman than Caesar. Still, as the coloured craze spreads, there are ever more classes for Cappy to contest at local shows, so one judge is bound to love him as much as Dora herself.

Miss Peculiar Priorities

YVONNE has Sergio Grasso riding boots, a tailor-made jacket and a lorry worth £25,000. Why she invests this sort of money on Splodge is anyone's guess.

Admittedly, he has a sweet temperament and eyelashes to die for. But 15 years' service at the local riding school – from where he was bought – has ruined his mouth, put him off serpentines for life, and achieving a 'soft and supple' outline is something he only acquiesces to at the end of a four-day intensive residential dressage clinic.

Yvonne has tried everything to bring Splodge up to prelim standard – Myler bits, an Albion dressage saddle, gait analysis and iridology. She once came third in a riding club competition performing her test on zero contact and a very long rein, success that fuelled a dressage frenzy. Splodge thus finds pictures of Salinero and Rusty glued up in his stable 'to inspire him' and is dragged to every clinic in the county. Yvonne's regular instructor begs her to consider trading the lorry for a trailer and reinvesting the loot in something with natural impulsion.

'Oh, but I could never part with Splodge,' says Yvonne, aghast. 'And I've a new bit on order that might just be the answer…'

The Not-So-First Horse

MUMMY has just bought Tilly her first horse. Tilly will go to Badminton one day, but is currently aiming for junior regional novices. High Jinks is Roger Federer on four legs — together, he and Tilly will win everything. True, High Jinks has yet to prove himself at the highest level, but, rest assured, he is 16.3hh of Thoroughbred potential. After all, he came with the tag: '20 BE points, professionally produced, double clear from here to kingdom come, will go far with junior/young rider', and that devastating seal of excellence: 'POA'.

Tilly's first lesson is something of a letdown when High Jinks refuses a cross-pole – three times. It is deemed too small for such a noble beast. Cross-country schooling goes little better. Tilly flounders in the water, while a dry-hoofed High Jinks glares from the step in.

The ground is to blame, but Tilly's mummy scratches their novice entries and downgrades to intro: 'Just until you get the hang of each other.'

At the event, High Jinks narrowly escapes elimination for having no chance after wading through five show jumping fences. He then takes a permanent objection to cross-country fence three. Tilly leaves the event long before her Pony Club rival wins – on a loaned 15hh 18-year-old cob.

The Eventing Baby

MOLLY is swaddled in a Newmarket rug and propped up in her ergonomic buggy, with two lurchers tethered to its frame. She is only two months old but looking at the scoreboard intently. Mummy – who hacked out the morning Molly was born and again two days after – is competing two pre-novices, three novices and an intermediate, 'just to get back into the swing of things'.

Molly already has a miniature piebald pony, Applejack, at the horse trials as a companion. He's in disgrace after getting loose and running amok in the lorry park.

Back at the lorry, Granny thrusts a smoked salmon sandwich into Molly's tiny pink mitts, wets her lips with champagne and gives her Mummy's mobile phone to play with. Molly would kill for a glug of warm milk. Later she is the focus of the prize-giving, perched on Mummy's hip and usurping the organiser's speech with whoops and squawks. When Mummy is presented with her rosette, Molly grabs Sir Cholmondely Whittingfeather's chubby finger and gurgles a toothless grin.

'I think we'll be seeing a bit more of this little one in the future,' he prophesies.

The Tackshop Terror

SHIRLEY has worked at Trimblemoor Trot-In Saddlery for almost 15 years. Business continues to thrive, in spite of her curt manner with customers – 'If you're going showing, you just can't save on a jacket. It'll have to be this one. Yes, you might bake, but the fit's gooooorgeous…' and 'My God, do you call that a hat? I'm surprised you're still alive. You'll need one of these now for Pony Club, and this endurance model is great for hacking in the summer.'

Shirley knows her taupe from her fawn, lemon from custard and caramel from coffee, and can tell if a fabric is two-, four- or no-way stretch from 20 paces. She tells clients straight how big their bum looks in joddies: 'Sorry love. They do nothing for your cellulite. I'm afraid you've no option but to try the Pikeurs. They'd make Dawn French look svelte.'

Trot-In Saddlery's owner is not quite sure whether it's thanks to Shirley's endearing honesty, or a need to escape further public embarrassment, that clients pay up and gallop out. Either way, profits are up 15% year-on-year, and Shirley is getting an espresso machine in the back office as a thank you.

STABLE STEREOTYPES

The Riding Holiday Fanatic

'I ASKED the travel agent about that Caribbean cruise you mentioned,' says Fiona. 'But – would you believe it – I had a look on the web and discovered you can get a fortnight on a ranch in Montana for only £750 extra, each. So I booked it.'

Her husband, Ian, nods resignedly.

Isn't it enough that he puts in 60 hours a week in mergers and acquisitions in order to finance his wife's horse habit without having to spend his precious free time around the damned animals too?

Within an hour of arriving in the States, Fiona is speaking with a faint American twang and discussing chinks and loping like she's been wrangling all her life.

After the first 12 hour bovine round-up, Ian is covered in blisters and has developed a gait John Wayne would be proud of. Fiona, brimming with enthusiasm, suggests buying a reining horse when they get back to the UK. Mentally totting up the cost of this new whim – and all the associated tack and lessons – Ian sighs, and follows her back into the ranch house.

Max the Footie Fan

MAX can hardly contain his excitement – but he will, of course, being a police horse. He's just heard they're off to Chelsea on Saturday for crowd control. Yes! Max, you see, is the biggest Blues fan on four legs.

He'll be hyped on Saturday morning, doing press ups in the straw before getting geared up for Stamford Bridge. Fortunately, Max's mounted officer understands the obsession and will keep him calm with some well-timed praise before kick-off.

At 2.15pm, Max will take up his position in line, eyeing up the crowds for troublemakers en route to the stands, his back right hoof propped and poised.

From 3pm, he will stand stock still, ears pricked for the full 90min, so as not to miss any roars from the crowds as the Blues score a 'screamer'.

His drooping bottom lip will flap as he chants: 'Blue is the colour, football is the game…', and he'll have a bet with the next horse in line as to who'll be man of the match – his oats are on Drogba.

Then comes the best bit, when the hoards of rowdy supporters pour out of the stadium towards the tube. Never mind the noisy mob, the pushing and the shoving, Max will be in his element listening to the commentary from those beer-swigging experts. Bring it on!

The Winter-Weary Livery Yard Manager

THIS winter has been a record-breaker at the yard Heather manages. Not only have her chilblains never throbbed so much, but it's been wetter and muckier than she can remember and virtually every full livery is a grey with a penchant for mud baths.

Naturally, their owners are the hardy sort that won't let a few feet of sludge get in the way of a good day's hunting or team chasing. Mind you, Heather has more time for this lot than the 'all gear, no idea' DIYers who start every sentence with 'Can you just show me how…?' and clog up the place with rugs and travel boots for mollycoddled mules who never venture further than the bridle path at the bottom of the lane.

Although she's fed up with the physical slog, it's preferable to placating moaning clients or motivating the silly girls that start work thinking it's going to be all pony rides in the sun. No wonder she smokes like a chimney.

Heather's social life isn't much rosier – it's hard to find a boyfriend when the scent of sweaty horse seems to stick to your skin.

What keeps her going is the dream of being William Fox-Pitt's competition groom. In the meantime, the thought of spring and a few dry days will just have to do.

The Distracted Fence Judge

DIANA had assured Amanda that fence judging was a breeze: 'A lovely day out for the children.' But a couple of hours in and Amanda is suffocating under the pressure.

Alarm bells should have rung during the briefing when the terrifying woman in charge started talking about paramedics and broken necks – Amanda assumed that bit was for the first aiders, so switched off. While initially dismayed to find her fence was miles from anywhere, given the chaos that's ensued, she's grateful for the privacy.

Amanda was busy unloading the gargantuan picnic from the boot – the children were already complaining about being bored and hungry – when the first horse came around. By the time she'd remembered the whistle, found the walkie-talkie and filled in the sheet a further five had gone flying through. This sent the dogs into a frenzy. They've been maypole dancing around the tow bar ever since and require unravelling at regular intervals.

Eventually, Amanda starts to feel on top of things so disappears into the car for the corkscrew. She emerges to find a riderless horse galloping towards her. Gripped by panic, she frantically waves every flag she's been given – one has to be the right colour, surely – while blasting on the whistle. Where's the wretched walkie-talkie?

'Oh bollocks,' cries Amanda, fishes out her mobile and dials 999.

The Teaser

PIP, teaser at the Plushmore Park Stud, is the sort of witty, funny bloke who chats up the girls only to find that they always go off with his better-looking mates who appear at the last minute. This is how he got his name – he's forever being pipped at the post.

Although it might seem a thankless task, Pip realises he's on to a pretty good thing. How else would a scruffy little Welsh mountain pony get to flirt with so many well-bred, lithe-legged ladies? He does suffer the odd kick and bite for his troubles, but Pip is a hardy soul. Plus, from time to time he is rewarded for the effort with which he beavers away with a roll in the hay with one of Plushmore's foster mares.

Unlike the stud's celebrated stallions, Pip enjoys a carefree, jack-the-lad existence – he's a free man, living out, eating what he fancies and never having to worry about what his mane and coat look like or being made to stand on show for hours at open days while the punters assess his talents.

On that front, Pip retaliates against any cheap 'Pipsqueak' or 'all mouth, no trousers' jibes by stomping a sizeable cobby hoof, glancing pointedly at the Thoroughbred stallions' fine little feet, and sniggering, 'You know what they say about shoe size, boys?'

The Good-Looking Whipper-in

EVER since fresh-faced Charlie arrived at the kennels, the ladies of the Lustmore hunt have been hot under the collar. None of them can resist the handsome whipper-in's permanently flushed cheeks and excellent seat. Charlie's ability to turn both hounds and heads hasn't gone unnoticed by the wizened huntsman, who dishes out frequent tongue-lashings in the hope of keeping the cheeky whippersnapper in line. However, all this has achieved is Charlie garnering more support from the girlies.

Young beauties in their first season out of ratcatcher try to cosy up covert-side, while the more matronly followers are in no doubt that the 'charming boy' needs mothering. Contrary to what they imagine, 'poor little Charlie' doesn't spend every night in his cottage polishing buttons and boots with just a mug of cocoa for

company. Rather, he's the life and soul of the Young Farmers. The stammering and inability to hold a gal's gaze that the Lustmore ladies mistake for bashfulness, are more likely caused by dehydration and a thumping head. But, with the hunt ball looming, Charlie's luck is in – he'll be pursued and cornered by a bitch pack, and it will require all his cunning to escape with his unblemished reputation in tact and avoid running home with his tail between his legs.

The Ambitious Amateur

'BUT why didn't he win?' demands Felicity Bigge-Pugh of the judge, who is shuffling determinedly sideways towards the collecting ring so he can make good his escape.

'He went perfectly,' Felicity continues. 'He's in super condition and he stood stock-still.'

The judge mutters something, sotto voce.

'WHAT?' Felicity, still astride Masons Hill Drummer Boy, pursues the judge out of the ring.

'He wrong-legged on both corners,' the judge repeats, blushing to the edges of his bowler. 'And he's carrying too much condition.'

'WHAAT!' Felicity is incensed. 'He's a heavyweight hunter! Of course he's carrying condition.'

By now, however, the safety of the officials' tent is but feet away and the judge, sensing sanctuary, gets rather brave.

'It's bone he should have, not fat,' he says, retreating gratefully. 'If you look at the professionals' horses, you'll see the difference in the topline.'

'WHAAAT!' Rising several decibels, Felicity's screech threatens to burst the judge's eardrums. 'That's what this is all about, isn't it? It's because I'm just an amateur, not a famous face!'

The Wait-Listed Eventer

KATE is on the Badminton waiting list. This would be her first year at 'the great event' and she's desperate to gallop round the famous cross-country track on her horse, Jumptoit.

Every day, before she's even swapped her pyjamas for jodhpurs, she gets on the internet and checks the Badminton website to see if anyone has withdrawn. Kate has worked out the likely percentage of withdrawals based on the past 20 years of data – this took her almost a week.

She's even been through the International Equestrian Federation (FEI) record of every horse accepted, checking for any time off which could signify an injury, which might recur and give her a chance of a run.

When she has a moment to spare from her calculations, Kate is keeping Jumptoit fit for his big Badminton debut. But her unhorsey sister Emma thinks Kate would stand a better chance if she went on a diet herself – she's been telling all her friends Kate can't go to Badminton because she's on the weight list.

The Classifieds Code-Breaker

READING *The Daily Telegraph* obits, Jackie laments she was born 65 years too late. She should have been that seam-stockinged code-breaker at Bletchley Park, sharing her desk with dashing wingcos – all moustache and ready wit – rather than wasting her talents grafting with Neville in accounts – all dandruff and halitosis.

She escapes her spreadsheet tedium by zapping through *The Times* crossword and the 'fiendish' grade sudoku, but her most acute pleasure comes from deciphering the *Horse & Hound* classifieds every Thursday. Jackie isn't actually looking for another horse – her darling Kit Kat is more than capable of 2ft 6in – but she adores finding the 'truth' behind the ads.

'Bucks a little' is rapidly translated as 'rears often'. 'Really tries to please' is dismissed as 'always comes seventh'. 'Suit confident

rider?' she scoffs. More like total lack of brakes.

Her scorn reaches a peak when her finger stops on a 16hh chestnut gelding described as a 'perfect gentleman'. Wasn't that the exact phrase the ghastly Brian had used about himself when Jackie had gone though her spell of dating through the personal columns? Still, at least this horse's owner fessed up to the gelding bit – unlike Brian.

The email pings another meeting in her manager's grey-walled office and she shoves *H&H* in her bag. She'd love another horse, and she'd love a lover. But Jackie has become, like the pony she first owned, irreversibly spooked.

The Mobile Cafe Owner

'RAIN'S clearing,' thinks Sue brightly as she wipes down her plastic chairs and tables before filling up the mustard and ketchup bottles from the drums out the back.

Catering hadn't really occurred to Sue before her life AD – After Derek. They'd met at a corporate do at Goodwood where he'd quickly moved from offering her a second glass to a ride in his Triumph Herald. Then, he seemed attractively wacky despite the brown shoes, but she learnt over long years that his passion for chrome and carburettors far outweighed her love for him. Still, if she'd finally lost out to a four-wheeled mistress at least those endless vintage car rallies gave her the idea for the café.

The first customer to The Feed Bucket rolls up at 8.15, a tiny tot with ribboned plaits and big smile demanding a 'quarter-pounder with extra cheese please'. Soon Sue is juggling sizzling bacon, hot cuppas and huge slices of chocolate cake, which she makes herself.

She's been on the horse circuit for three years, likes the organisers and knows many faces. The profits are meagre and she'd probably do better in her old job in accounts – with none of the 'fun' of extricating her van from a sodden field in the middle of 'summer'. But Sue loves the gypsy life and her customers, especially the children, and often let's them have a packet of Polos when their money doesn't quite cover it.

On the haul to the next show she thinks how happy she'd have been as a mother. But then she arrives, sees all those kids with their ready smiles and happily flips over another burger.

The Notorious Navigator

AMELIA'S bottom is not what it was. What was once firm and springy has now been labelled rotten by her husband. She should get it fixed – we refer, of course, to her trailer's floor – thus saving her from having to cadge lifts to shows, but fat chance of that with the school fees.

Such concerns never trouble Claire, her stable friend from her pre-teens. But then nothing ever has, thinks Amelia bitterly – least of all morals. While Amelia was slogging away at business studies, Claire was dropping Es almost as fast as her knickers before she netted Ed the banker. Claire now blazes round the event circuit in an EquineEquippe horsebox that's bigger than Amelia's cottage.

'It's ridiculous for just two horses,' purrs Claire, 'though I do find the little bed so handy' – an observation that brings a silent 'I bet' to Amelia's lips.

Claire has offered to box her cobby mare to a one-dayer 'just up the road'. Amelia's pretty sure it's near Godalming – or was it Guildford? Anyway, it's somewhere along the M3 and she's scribbled the instructions on a Post-It. It's a shame she left it by the phone as they realise it should have been the A3. There's no map, so it's down to the Sat Nav, into which Amelia keeps punching horse trials under 'local points of interest'. Now 20 minutes late for her start time, Claire finally succumbs to the automaton screaming 'Turn right, turn right' and swings the pantechnicon into a squiggle-sized road.

It's residential, with cars parked on both sides and a van driver behind blasting his horn. In grim silence, Amelia and Claire drive towards Guildford city centre.

Bramble the Foxhound

'*AND* now, girls and boys, ladies and gentlemen, please give a big welcome to THE BLANKSHIRE FOXHOUNDS!'

'Hell's teeth, here we go again,' sighs Bramble, as he puts in a deep-throated 'whoof, whoof' and wags his stern to show willing. In the season, he's Charlie the huntsman's favourite. Bramble might not have the cat-pawed, level beauty that wins Royal Peterborough rosettes, but he's honest, never gives tongue till he's sure and has the brains to cast wide without instruction. But galloping round a county showring on a baking summer afternoon? No, thanks.

Three-quarters round the circuit Bramble spots a gap between two toddlers licking ice-creams. A quick check that Charlie's looking the other way and he's through the crowd quicker than a New Zealand fly-half. It's time for a scent check and an instant decision — the veniburger stall or the home-produce tent?

Bramble shimmies through the legs like a greased eel, ignoring the general cooing and attempts to pet him. He sidles into the tent and his nose locks on to a savoury smell with the accuracy of a surface-to-air missile. A small child is tugging at his parent's arm with one hand while a large, barely-touched sausage-roll dangles in the other. Seconds later, Bramble is exiting fast with a bleating child in his wake.

Charlie's sounding the recall, so he doubles his pace and heads straight to the ring via the president's tent. He spots a large florid lady in an equally florid dress, holding forth over a glass of Pimm's.

A quick cock of the leg, a satisfying shriek of female outrage and he's back with the pack, another mission accomplished.

Dionne Breeze 2008.

The Man Hunter

IT'S like the soundtrack from the old *Hound of the Baskervilles,* but instead of Basil Rathbone stuffing his pipe, Sam's sparking up a Marlboro Light.

Her problem, as ever, is the lack of a reliable man. She did try a girl once but it wasn't nearly as good. They just don't have the stamina. The East Vale Bloodhounds really need a proper chap to hunt, preferably one of those Loughborough physical education types who go like a startled stag.

A knackered Fiat scorches in and her runner bales out in a flurry of shorts and apologies. The hounds start baying again and practise their fierce criminal-catching faces. No one's convinced. It might have worked for their ancestors, who had the best time tracking down escaped Dartmoor prisoners, but this lot are as soft as ice cream.

Sam's now in her third season as field master and she gathers up the usual mix of revved-up kids and curious foxhunters and explains the form, while their student zooms round laying his own human trail.

Twenty minutes later and the hounds' deep music tolls through the valley. Sam tries to put in a couple of false casts, but the scent is scorching and so is the pace. The whole field is almost at the gallop and, in due course, the hounds tumble on to their man caught up in a hedge.

The experience has left the followers resembling the Light Brigade — after the charge. Sam has another fag and gives her man a bottle of Lucozade as he prepares for the next run. She reckons this one will do it at least three times, which isn't bad. Though that very fit Loughborough student managed five, she recalls with a smirk.

The Corporate Polo Guest

NO bird-watcher could rival Helen at twitching, though her bible isn't the *Collins Guide to British Birds* but a well-thumbed *Hello!*

'Ohmigod, look, by the Aston Martin, isn't that? It is! It's Kate Moss!' Head swivelling like a U-boat periscope, Helen then spots an impossibly long pair of brown legs accompanying a bloke with the stature and haircut of a Polish bantam.

'Quick, just behind — Penny Lancaster and Rod Stewart!'

When Gary, head of software procurement at work, asked Helen to the polo she'd accepted at once, having long admired the game through the pages of Jilly Cooper's bonkbuster.

'Of course, at half-time we have to go and tread in the duvets,' she explains to Gary as he drains a warm glass of Pimm's.

'OK,' he mumbles, 'but why do they keep changing ends every time they score a goal?"

Jilly, always so detailed on scoring in the romantic sense, failed to impart this info to Helen and she isn't listening anyway, having seen a D&G dress mostly filled with a cleavage like a black ski run.

'It's Jordan, or rather Katie Price, as she prefers to be known,' says Helen proudly. 'She was into ponies same time as me.'

Jordan's name has an almost Pavlovian effect on Gary.

'Will she be doing this duvet business, too?' he asks, rather too casually.

'Of course!' replies Helen. 'Everyone does.'

In the Cartier tent, implausibly beautiful women drape round men heavy in both Rolexes and accents. They remain firmly inside their champagned cocoon while Helen and Gary wander like wildebeest, seeking an errant divot.

The Tetrathlon Dad

HE stands alone, the bull in the herd.

'More like a gelding among mares,' Henry thinks ruefully.

After the usual minotaur maze of back lanes and no signs – 'Why can't women organise signs?' – they've arrived at the area tetrathlon.

The car instantly empties, his children bolting off to their mates, his wife to talk non-stop pony with other mothers.

Henry takes the cased air-pistol and tries to find the shooting range. None of his wife's friends seems capable of putting a pellet into the gun right-side up, so he's been 'volunteered' to do the loading for half a dozen youths.

Trying to collect the targets he discovers, as usual, they've all been grabbed 'by a tall woman in a Puffa', a description that fits 95 per cent of the adult females present.He tracks her down and settles on the range with the first girl, a good rider, runner and swimmer. But shooting? The safest place is right in front of the target.

For the next two hours he's marooned there as his charges spray pellets with the accuracy of damp confetti and Henry's mind wanders to his friends, sailing off the Solent with a pub run planned at Cowes. At last the teenagers are emptying towards the swimming pool for the final phase where half a dozen mothers are already screaming hysterical encouragement to assorted Charlottes.

Returning to the car, Henry pours a lukewarm coffee and vows this really will be the last time. But then the teenagers bounce up with rosettes and seem reasonably pleased to see him. One even thanks him for loading for her. In six weeks there's another tet and somehow, despite everything, Henry finds he's scribbling the date into his diary.

The Silver Ring and Royal Enclosure Girls

JASMINE'S wobbly and it's only 10am.

'Nothing to do with this,' she giggles as she drains another glass of Buck's Fizz. And she's almost right – it would take a Chinese State Circus acrobat to stay steady on her soaring heels. They're cream, a perfect match with her pencil skirt, jacket and cocktail hat. She bought the lot in Monsoon – it's a bit more understated than Jasmine's usual high-rise mini, but she knows from *Now* magazine that Coleen wore something almost identical to Ascot last year.

'Sides, you can always accessorise, can't you girls?' she shrieks, as she undoes another button and lets the Wonderbra'd occupants surface like synchronised seals.

At Waterloo station, Charlotte checks the clock anxiously. Demure in blue with her Royal Enclosure badge barely encompassing her double-barrelled surname, she scans the throng for Piers, her current squeeze with husband potential. They travel First and join Mummy and Daddy's picnic at Car Park 2 before embarking on the assault course cycle of paddock, Royal Enclosure and Pimms bar. Charlotte can hardly move for old friends from Heathfield and Cirencester, most of whom seem to be sporting rocks the size of Gibraltar on their left hands.

Jasmine has bumped into Carl, who wandered over to their gaggle bearing a bottle of Moët and an expectant grin. Somehow, she has accepted his offer of a glass and a lift home.

Charlotte lost Piers temporarily after he met Fiona, a long-legged 'old friend from St Andrews'. She looks over the racecourse and wonders idly why anyone would bother attending Ascot without Royal Enclosure tickets.

Jasmine doesn't give a hoot which stand she's in. She's at Ascot with her well-oiled mates and Carl is fit. Unlike Charlotte, this lady's day promises an exciting finish.

The Camp Commander

'EINSTEIN was right,' thinks Lucy. 'Time is relative. And somewhere it's got to be sundown.'

She uncorks the warm pinot grigio with a shrug, fills a plastic cup and drains it in one.

Her day began at 6am, when some of the younger brutes decided to pull out the pegs from their friends' tents. The clamour spread to the whole camp and by 6.45am Lucy was trying to supervise fried breakfasts, stop an impromptu bareback race and blockade the boys from 'accidentally' wandering into the girls' showers.

Naturally, all of this would be easy with helpers. Naturally, there aren't any. OK, she has Amanda and Rosie, both veterans of Pony Club camp. But some of the new mothers? Lucy crumples her cup in silent fury.

They whinge that their kids aren't in the right ride. Yell at their children. Complain about the instructors. And they disappear faster than a dropped fiver as soon as there's a job to be done.

She pulls a piece of bracken from her hair. The kids use all the hot water and there's bugger-all chance of a shower until she returns to civilisation. But there're still two nights to go and she checks that the mega candle-power torch is fully charged for her impersonation of the Colditz commandant. Last night's patrol found a pile of boys and girls dossing in the same tent, two teenagers bouncing around in bikinis and another two singing Abba's greatest hits — at 2am.

'Lord knows what the parents will think,' Lucy mutters aloud. 'But since they're not damn well here, who cares?'

She pours another tumbler of wine and shouts to Amanda to grab another bottle.

The Foster Mum

CONSTANCE was most definitely built for comfort rather than speed, something she's provided to countless flimsy-looking Thoroughbred foals over the years.

But listening to this season's little upstart brag about the prowess of his parents, grandparents and great-grandparents is testing her legendary reserves of patience, especially the relentless questions about her own indistinct Irish heritage: 'Do you know my cousins over in Tipperary?' he pipes up repeatedly.

In spite of these inquiries, this generously proportioned skewbald mare is given the cold shoulder by her cheeky young charges – unless they are in need of refreshment or to shelter from the wind behind her substantial flank. And the Thoroughbred mares aren't much friendlier.

'Just goes to show that good breeding doesn't guarantee manners,' mutters Constance to a fellow foster mare, the equally buxom Bridget, as a recent Oaks winner flounces past with her foal, noses aloft.

While Constance may not frolic in the field with the others' grace – it's been years since her four feathered feet left the ground – she takes pride in the athletic performances of her adopted foals and the role she played in raising them when their own mothers couldn't step up to the plate.

'These girls might think they're yummy mummies with their glossy manes and lithe limbs but what is there to cuddle up to?' she tuts to Bridget between hearty mouthfuls of grass.

The Unstable Companion

'*AND* there's four furlongs to go…and it's neck and neck…and Horace is coming in on the inside…and it's Horace by a nose!'

He tugs at another mouthful of grass and dreams of Ascot. Horace, lacking a looking glass, has no idea he's a Shetland. His companion, Mercury Quicksilver, is a chestnut Thoroughbred, polished in coat and poise, and worth several high-hedge funds. But as far as Horace is concerned, he's just lanky, with a silly name. Both of them know who's the paddock boss. And the real winner.

Horace still recalls the crowd's clamour when he nailed the Shetland Grand National at Olympia. Whereas Mercury, for all his primping, has yet to better a Redcar fourth. But did his former owners appreciate his Olympian heights? Did they hell. He braces his bottom against the fence and has a good scratch. Their ghastly child dumped him in favour of an overheight bay that could 'jump like a gazelle'.

'Pity it looked like a hippo,' mutters Horace, before smiling at his

success in marking the upstart's flanks with his signature bite. But did that really deserve being exiled to Lambourn? At least the wannabe racehorses will now appreciate his advice.

And next time Mercury's boxed up, he'll slip in and show the world who exactly is their new Red Rum – albeit a rather short one.

STABLE STEREOTYPES

The Secret Hay Buyer

CHLOE'S mobile phone rings out the 'gone away', and she wishes she'd chosen something a little less robust, a bit more Four Seasons. It's her third call of the day and every time she's had to abandon her fellow fence judge and nip behind the bushes. She returns looking slightly flushed.

'Who was that, Chloe?' asks Amanda, all innocence.

'Oh, just one of the children trying to find their cross-country number,' Chloe replies unconvincingly, her voice breaking slightly.

'So, not that rather dashing farrier you've just acquired. Greg, isn't it?' drawls Amanda with a quite unnecessary wink.

'Cheeky cow,' thinks Chloe, but she cannot tell a single soul the truth. One word and her supply will be jeopardised. It was bad enough last year, but finding good hay this summer has been a nightmare. With wheat at £165 a ton, every farmer within 10 miles has ploughed up the pasture and put it to cereals. And those who did grow hay have been hit by the monsoon weather.

Finally, she's tracked down a good source of meadow hay, rather than the thistle-strewn muck Caroline conned her into taking last year. Greg gave her the source after she took him down a cuppa while wearing a dangerously low-scooped top. She'd even bent down deliberately to hold a hind hoof. But if a decent helping of cleavage produces a stable full of decent hay, she should worry.

Brian the farmer is delivering it tomorrow. She did ask, casually, if anyone else in the riding club had contacted him. Apparently not. Chloe blows her whistle as another rider approaches and decides Brian might also like a nice cup of tea. And perhaps she'll don that low-scooped top once again.

The New Master

OVER breakfast, he stops abruptly at the newspaper headline. 'Just one kiss could prove fatal,' it warns. Didn't Judith have a nut allergy? Or was that just another of his wife's not-tonight devices? He looks down at the peanut butter – he'll spread it good and thick and give her a fond farewell kiss.

Adrian never had these murderous thoughts about his wife prior to the fateful dinner party when she volunteered him for the new mastership.

'It'll be so good for our social lives,' she cooed. 'Don't you know MFHs stand above MPs in social precedence?'

'So do most forms of invertebrate,' he'd slurred back, but it was too late. He'd been nobbled. Granted, he enjoyed the odd day out with hounds. But mastership?

'Nothing to it, old chap,' Rupert, the senior master, had purred over the port after Judith had sealed the deal. 'I'll do the paperwork. And Frank will be the field master. If you could just help out with the…'

The sentence was left open, rather like the chequebook now lying on the breakfast table. Adrian picks up the pen and reluctantly writes out his contribution to the hunt coffers.

'Well, I just hope Judith damn well thinks it's worth it,' he sighs.

He then remembers the last meet and the lovely Charlotte, who looked incredibly foxy in her new fitted breeches and, as his memory serves him, was rather too long in shaking hands. He picks up the pen again, adds another zero to the cheque and heads into the kitchen to find another jar of peanut butter.

The Top Rider's Terrier

AS soon as the ramp comes down on Bullet's owner's sickeningly swanky horsebox, the pocket-rocket terrier proves he's been aptly named. Within seconds of shooting out with the velocity of a cruise missile, he's causing carnage, ricocheting off everything from water buckets to bemused horses.

If this spectacle isn't sufficient to herald his arrival, the hullabaloo that follows Bullet wherever he goes can't be ignored – to the irritation of those competitors trying to have a few minutes' quiet contemplation before going into the ring.

However, at least the racket serves as an early-warning siren to all those thinking of setting up their picnic – barrel-chested Bullet is a renowned cool-box burglar. He no doubt needs the extra calories because he's forever bouncing up and down on the spot like a pooch on a pogo stick.

The box park heaves a collective sigh of relief when Bullet's owner goes off to walk the show jumping course. Here, the terrible terrier entertains himself by disrupting those trying to count strides and work out which corners can be cut. Some riders put his owner's success down to the 'Bullet effect'.

But for all he might puff himself up like a pint-sized prize-fighter, Bullet's a closet softie, liking nothing more than to curl up on a warm knee for the journey home after a good day's hell-raising.

The Farmer-Trainer

LIKE most farmers, Arthur never misses the farming forecast, but foremost in his mind is not how the weather might affect matters agricultural, but its impact on the going at Garthorpe and, crucially, who will be exercising his two point-to-pointers that morning.

If it's really filthy, Arthur will find some pressing farming issues to attend to and it will be left to his wife Mary to take the reins. In fact, Mary does most of the dirty work but happily so, as she's as passionate about pointing as her spouse. On racedays, the horses' coats gleam when they're loaded into the cattle wagon.

They always look the picture of health but never win best turned-out because Arthur doesn't believe in ostentation such as plaiting or unnecessary nonsense like nosebands. While never likely to set the racing world alight, Arthur's horses always run honestly and, most importantly, give him and the missus some smashing days' hunting.

Whatever the result, there's always a large throng around the couple's lorry catching up on the latest gossip, moaning about feed prices and enjoying the hospitality – Mary's spreads are legendary. Arthur's in his element with cheeks flushed from excitement, not to mention a string of whisky macs. Needless to say, it's a safe bet Mary will be behind the wheel for the trip back to the farm.

The University Surplus

'*A 16.2hh* 10-year-old talented eventer, good to hack, handle, 100 per cent in every way – a true gent. Knock-down price as no rider.'

Eric is just one of the many identikit riderless horses on the market come September and Mum isn't hopeful she'll find a buyer before Rosanna disappears off to university, not to be heard from again until the Christmas holidays.

Then the unthinkable happens – the perfect new owners turn up for a viewing. The middle-aged couple are instantly charmed by Eric who, eyeing them up suspiciously, notices the well-worn boots of the woman and the muscular legs of the man. These two could mean hard work, he ponders.

'He doesn't buck, does he?' enquires the woman. As Mum reassures her he is the perfect gentleman, a plan begins to form.

A few nips, an interesting performance on the end of the lead rope, several unrequested and exuberant flying changes and a couple of gravity-defying leaps later, Eric watches the couple leave, accusations of false advertising flying over their shoulders as they flee the yard.

He's heard all about these university horses, turned away for nine months of the year. He can already hear Mum mixing dinner in the feed room and nudges her gently as she emerges, the perfect gent once more. Yes, Eric thinks, snatching at a mouthful of hay from a bulging rack before inspecting the clean bed of shavings, this could all work out rather well.

The First-Time Dressage Writer

'RHYHTM'. 'Rhyhtm'. 'Rhythym'. Whichever way Judy writes it, it still looks wrong. She wishes she'd had the foresight to bring a dictionary, as well as a flask of coffee and a blanket. The indoor school is absolutely freezing.

'Seven. Nice rhythm,' says Roberta, the judge, in a stage whisper that can be heard, quite clearly, up in the gallery.

That word again, Judy muses as she scribbles, wondering how long she'll be able to keep writing anyway, what with her hands slowly turning blue.

She'd stumbled upon the idea of doing some dressage writing when competing at her last one-day event of the season. The judge that day had been cosily sitting in her 4x4, sharing endless coffees and insights with her writer, or so Judy had imagined anyway. Writing for a dressage judge would expand her knowledge, give something back to the horseworld, and may even help her in her never-ending quest to finally get a sub-50 dressage score when the eventing season kicked off again next March.

'Straight up centre line, square halt,' says Roberta while Judy frantically scrawls the comments from the medium trot, three movements earlier. 'Nice horse, shame about the rider. Don't write that bit though, ha ha!"

Judy hastily scores out her last few words, and then hands over the test sheet so Roberta can add her comments.

'Oh dear,' says Roberta, kindly. 'You've spelt rhythm wrong again. Never mind, there's 25 horses still to go, plenty of time to get it right.'

The Hunt Policeman

CRACKLE CRACKLE, crackle. 'Oscar Foxtrot Tango, proceeding now to Blackfriars Farm as instructed. Charlie Foxtrot Oscar out.' Crackle, crackle.

'OK Steve, let's go and show our faces,' grins Gary, as he swings the 4x4 out into the lane, making sure there's room for the three children atop their ponies. Each gives a cheery wave.

This is the coppers' best job of the week – a day in the countryside. They're both keen shots and pick up locally, but today they've swapped their usual breeks and gumboots for snazzy – if rather SAS-style – black overalls, high-laced boots and baseball caps. Steve thinks it makes them 'look like something out of Hot Fuzz', but they're being paid to watch hounds – what's there to complain about?

They both took part in the Countryside March, but the law is the law and they have turned up at the meet to enforce it. At first, they accepted an early bacon roll and coffee from the hunt supporters. Now, however, they pack their own as they decided that this wasn't quite impartial.

The master stands in his stirrups, nods a good morning to the two officers and booms a reminder to the field that they are of course hunting within the law.

Hounds move off and Gary shifts the 4x4 into low ratio and joins the trail of car followers. Their 'elf 'n' safety' officer has reminded

them not to follow on foot through the woods in case of potential accidents – which is a shame as it's the cep-collecting season.

At 3pm, their shift ends and they swing back to the station after a cracking day, their departure noted by every mounted follower.

The Horse Sale Novice

CHRISTA can hardly contain her excitement. Years of Pony Club eventing and hunting have now green-lighted her way into the world of the horse professional — and hand-in-hand with this graduation goes a trip to the Irish sales.

Just like Dick Whittington's London, the streets are paved with gold in this Irish market town. Now that she is a professional, the business of spotting a gem and selling it to an amazed buyer is her aim in life.

Loathe to head out alone, Christa attaches herself to Faye, a local dealer who often seems to emerge victorious with at least a handful of hunters and a brace of youngsters with potential. Inspired by Faye's tales of success, Christa has emptied the piggy bank and arrives amid the mighty confusion more than a little shell-shocked.

A quick look at the catalogue points her in the right direction. A glance at the back end ('bottom like a cook', Faye mutters prophetically) denotes the way and an informative chat with a blue-eyed boy called Vince confirms the location of the Holy Grail of horses.

As Christa sees her glittering prospect on to the transporter, she decides to name him 'Irish Charm' – not a little swayed by those persuasive blue eyes. It is only when a rotund cob comes off the lorry at the other end that Christa fears the charm may well and truly have rubbed off, probably somewhere in the middle of the Irish Sea. But not to worry, those blue eyes will see her heading across again next year.

The Pet Collector

SPACE is tight in Sheila's cottage and time non-existent in her life, with three horses, four dogs, two cats, a billy goat and a tame pheasant – but she would not want it any other way. Her social life is also a bit limited, too. Running home at regular intervals to let out an incontinent dog – Scruffy, the lurcher with a leak – doesn't make her the ideal dinner party guest, but that's life.

The horses aren't much help either. Having built three lovely stables to keep them snug all winter, Sheila rarely gets to ride. Poppy – bless her – is 28 and, despite the spirit being willing, the body is not anymore, while Teddy Edward is only 12hh (a 'gift' from an ex-boyfriend) and William is one of those accident-prone horses who spends more time off work than in.

Mind you, squeezing into the car and trailer on those days when William is raring to go can be a challenge because all the dogs want to sit on the front seat. And the time when Pete the pheasant hitched a lift to the summer show has gone down in local riding club history.

Her friends are concerned Sheila's waifs and strays are taking over her life, but she's happy – especially as they give her a good excuse to keep popping into the practice to consult Ben, her easy-on-the-eye and ever-patient vet.

The Nagsman

TOMMY groans and stares out of the window. It's pitch black, freezing cold and he has three to ride before breakfast, two of them confirmed bolters.

Tommy doesn't have his own yard and rarely has his own horse. His speciality is riding those troublesome steeds that nobody else will. It's not so much a job as a way of living, surviving hand to mouth, but with a reputation for performing wonders with the most wayward of horses.

By 6am Tommy will be at somebody's yard. Skilled fingers tack-up in a fraction of the time that it takes Keira, the girl groom. Her diploma in horse care is no competition for Tommy's 40 years of experience. He is treated with something akin to reverence among the hunting folk who have landed themselves with a nag who's a touch too hot to handle.

After one embarrassment too many, the infallible advice 'give Tommy a ring' can be heard in the hunting field. Having previously dismissed him as overrated, many red-faced riders cave in and make that call. When Tommy arrives at the yard of Arnie's owners, he looks as cool as a cucumber. As he saunters out of the yard, everybody waits.

An hour and a half later Tommy is back – in one piece – and Arnie looks like butter wouldn't melt.

'He's all right is this 'oss,' says Tommy, 'but he'll need to be taken in hand for a bit. I'll hunt him next Friday.' Meekly consenting, Arnie's owners can think of nothing they'd rather do. As Tommy leaves in his battered Fiesta, he allows himself a brief smile. A full season's hunting on Arnie looms who, after all, isn't so bad, just misunderstood — and another couple of unbelievers have joined the ministry.

The Road Trippers

THEY hit the road with the experienced cool of an Eddie Stobart driver. Janet swings the huge wheel round, missing the gateposts by at least 2in, and takes a swig of coffee from the Thermos mug. It's 6am, the road's empty. She shoves in the iPod lead and blasts out the theme from Convoy, the 1970s trucker film.

Pickle considers adding his yowl to Janet's karaoked 'They even had a bear in the air', but decides to resume his position of key navigator.

Of course, being a Jack Russell, it's hard for him to always give Janet the right instructions, but he's her constant companion throughout the team chase season.

'So, what did you think of Charlie then, Pickle?' she asks.

'Not much,' is the unbarked answer. Proper Jack Russells dislike being booted out of their rightful place in the mistress's bed by hairy boyfriends.

'Well, perhaps boyfriend is too strong a term,' thinks Pickle.

Men come and go in Janet's life. Always keen on her in stretch breeks, they're less so once they realise her utter commitment to her horse, her sport and, of course, Pickle.

Every weekend Janet is out, either team chasing or hunting, and after the third invitation to 'spend the weekend over at my place' declined, the boys tend to move on.

Janet discusses each new romantic rollercoaster with Pickle – a far better listener than her mother, who always bangs on about 'that nice Colin'. The JR lets her words wash over him as he considers the morning's entertainment.

He knows that in 15min they'll arrive and he can give that farm collie his really savage bark 'n' snarl routine – all from the safety of the horsebox cab. And then there's that nice little Norwich bitch of Janet's friend's Sue, attractively smelly at the last encounter.

The thought so tickles Pickle that he joins in the song's chorus – 'Convooooooy, Convooooy' – and notes that he's more in tune than Janet.

Breeze 2008.

The Point-to-Point Punter

'*ALWAYS* back the grey,' says Henry, tapping the side of his nose knowingly with a bony finger. 'If there's two, obviously it's void, but if there's three, back the outsider of them.'

Backing the 'outsider of three' is a good racing adage, and the only bit of Henry's frankly risible betting advice that carries any weight. While he's always to be seen flashing fivers – and tenners and sometimes even twenties – at the bookies, he is remarkably close-mouthed on his level of success.

'Ah, that would be telling,' he says, winking like a terrier with a tic.

What is even more telling is the growing collection of torn-up betting slips with which his ancient Volvo is awash. And the fact that, in the pub after the meeting, he is inclined to go for a cigarette or to answer the call of nature when it's his round.

Of course, betting – particularly on point-to-points – is not an exact science. But some of Henry's more outlandish tips seem to owe more to (ineffectual) witchcraft than any form of judgement

regarding pedigree and form. For example: 'Only bet on bays on alternate days.'

What? There is a strong suspicion he makes it up as he goes along.

But despite his dodgy 'tips' and disappearances at crucial times at the bar, Henry's natural charm and general good humour means he remains popular with his racegoing circle. And with the course bookies — who all wink like terriers with tics and tap their noses knowingly when he hoves into view…

The Show Jumping Mum

'GO on – faster! Turn! YES!'

Mum lets the stopwatch on which she times each round — after all, you can't rely on show centres to get it right — fall to her chest and punches the air in jubilation.

Rosie drops the barely puffing Mr Fabulous's reins as she leaves the arena, poles happily still in their cups despite a hairy moment, and pats his neck.

'Well, that turn was a bit bloody silly,' says Mum, as she stuffs the treasured pony with Polos, all her attention on the four-legged hero of the moment. 'Lucky for you it came off.'

The other mothers exchange smiles – they all know that had Rosie not attempted the turn and finished in second place, she would be getting moaned at more than this. No place for steady clears in that family.

Rosie sighs and looks around at the other competitors, being praised and fussed over, merely for staying on for once.

'What I wouldn't give for a mum like theirs,' she sighs inwardly.

The tannoy booms and Rosie leads the way back into the arena, taking her place at the head of the line-up.

'Although on second thoughts,' she reconsiders, eyeing the approaching ribbons and fat envelope with gleeful anticipation, 'perhaps mine isn't so bad.'

The Equestrian Novelist

CAROLINA is doing research for her latest novel, *A Roll in the Hay*. Blockbusting fiction and horses are a winning combination, as dear Jilly Cooper proved.

Carolina's publisher loves the idea of a novel set in the glitzy worlds of eventing, racing and mountain and moorland showing. Carolina has even decided to spend some of the book advance on a horse, to help her get to grips with the subject.

She's not finding it as easy as she'd expected though. Her hayfever is raging due to all the time she's spending in stables researching possible locations for romantic clinches.

The riders she interviews are being deliberately obtuse about which jodhpur brands come up the tightest fitting and which horsebox marque has the most pulling power. Nor is she convinced equestrianism is as glamorous as it was supposed to

be. Lady riders all seem to carry a strange whiff of mucking out, and their horses' bedrooms are a lot tidier than their own.

Carolina's own horse is eating its way through her advance and she has to wear two jumpers, a gilet, a Puffa and a Barbour just to keep warm at the yard. If anyone tried to remove all that in the name of seduction, they'd die of boredom first.

The Assistant Trainer

DAVID considers himself to be a bit like Prince Charles – waiting for the aged-P to drop off the perch so he can get the top job.

Having ploughed his 'A' levels and only got the tractor drivers' diploma at Cirencester – unfortunately, he inherited his mother's brains and his father's looks – he did the usual round of working for trainers in the US and Australia, a six-month stint with a top national hunt trainer, then home to Dad.

None of the stable girls can stand him. After a few pints in The Yard – the Newmarket pub he describes as his spiritual home – he thinks he has droit de seigneur.

Easily spotted in his red cords, David thinks he's pretty hot stuff. And training Group One winners is going to be a walk in the park. But when his father leaves him in charge and first lot doesn't pull out until David's hangover has receded, the wrong horses get worked. The old man blows his top and lets slip that he has never intended to hand over to David anyway – what kind of a fool does he think he is?

The Suave Man at the Gate

BRIAN can't recall how he got sucked into the glamorous world of traffic management, but the lunches – and hon secretary – of Little Piddling Horse Trials are so delicious that, incredibly, this is his 12th year.

It's not as brainless as it sounds. Queries vary wildly from, 'Please, we must have shade!' to 'I beg you, DON'T send us through the mud. We'll never get out!'

Dianne Breeze 2008.

Twenty years in stockbroking have taught Brian how to cloak disappointment with charm, and everyone who passes his gate mentally labels him 'Such a nice man'. He recognises timid towing mums, wild-eyed with panic at the thought they may have to reverse, and handles them gently. 'Park on the left, my dear, and you'll be able to pull forward to get out. Best of luck…'

Horse trials weather is unpredictable. Brian packs sun cream and a top-to-toe Dryzabone, whatever the forecast. Overall, he prefers it wet. His lungs don't get clogged with dust, his wife spoils him upon his return, and once he was able to cadge a lift home on the towing tractor.

The Trailer Repair Man

SUSIE rues the day she sent her trailer to Tony for a 'once over'. Six weeks and £800 later, it is still off the road awaiting parts. Tony phones her almost daily with updates she'd rather not hear.

'Listen, I've just looked under your floor mats and it isn't pretty…' and 'You know I said I thought I could rescue your wiring? Well I've got some bad news…'

Even getting divorced wasn't this stressful.

But 'I've started so I'll finish', becomes Susie's guiding principle until, cowering behind dark sunglasses to disguise her pained expression, she arrives to hand over £2,500 for fixing up a 10-year-old trailer that costs £3,500 to buy new.

Deciding a cross-country clinic is the thing to cheer herself up, Susie hitches up her outwardly unaltered trailer next day to find the horse refuses, point blank, to load.

STABLE STEREOTYPES

The Pony Club Lothario

AT 15 years old, Sebastian has a little black book longer than the *Yellow Pages*. When his mother sends in the cheque to confirm that Seb will be attending camp again that year, the District Commissioner gives a sigh of relief. His teenage fan club will undoubtedly cause her sleepless nights all week, but without him attendance would fall by half.

Seb wouldn't miss camp for the world, despite all those boring flatwork lessons. It's the easiest week of the year for him, thanks to his legion of admirers offering to feed his horse, muck out, groom, tack up and clean it afterwards.

Mid-morning he saunters down to the yard, yet still wins the best turned out prize five days in a row. Lessons are spent slouching in the saddle, frantically texting on his mobile whenever the instructor isn't looking.

Seb is hugely confident about winning the one-day event on the final day, even with the distraction of walking the show jumping course with 17 giggling girls trailing in his wake. If only one of them would memorise his dressage test for him, he'd be sorted.

Comedy Commentator

'*LADIES* and gentlemen, boys and girls, let's hear a big cheer now for…'

Since the Horse of the Year Show turned him down, Tony Smoothlie has carved a weekend career as a commentator of note – well, within the South Lincolnshire area, anyway. He's aching to introduce Whitakers, Skelly and Robert Smith to the spectators, even if they do ride all those unpronounceable warmbloods, for which he's taken a Berlitz course in basic Dutch in readiness.

But for now, he's confined to pre-novice and intro day at a local horse trials, and he is appalled to find someone has half-inched the taped electric organ blast he was going to play down his microphone every time someone jumped a clear round.

The Hon Sec blanches when he urges onlookers to start a Mexican wave: 'It's not the Olympics, you know Tony!'

But his keenness, punctuality and willingness to step in at the last minute mean she's stuck with him again this year.

Nearly 12 hours later, Tony is still glued to his microphone, desperate for a comfort break, and rather doubting the merits of this gig, when lo, his heart lifts. His opening gambit at the pub tonight is secured – when Zara Phillips canters into the ring on a novice.

Queen of the Yard

PHILIPPA is in a panic, her crown is at stake. Yard manager Emily has just told her that a new livery is coming today and she used to work for a top eventer. For the past couple of years Philippa has been the undisputed queen of the yard at Boggy Meadows Livery Stables, asked to consult on everything from thrush to thoroughpins.

She's spent many a happy hour looking on knowledgeably while her fellow liveries bandage on a poultice or a clip on a ticklish elbow, adding helpful comments which she's sure they really appreciate.

And she understands why Emily doesn't like her watching when she takes lessons in the outdoor school – she's, understandably, jealous of her extensive knowledge and worried she might slip up. As she bustles off to look for her headcollar again – it keeps disappearing and last time she found it on top of the hay bales – there are giggles from her fellow riders.

Yes, a new livery is coming to the yard and yes she did work at a top event yard… as a nanny.

The Reluctant Reader

IT took countless sulks, the threat of divorce and promises of no hot food for a month before John agreed to call Pamela's dressage test. Now he's missing the Formula One grand prix to stand in the driving rain, holding the sodden test sheet, bellowing out random letters of the alphabet so that dear Pam and Deecry Absouluut, her Dutch Warmblood, will know where to execute their endless changes of rein.

And is she grateful? Is she hell.

'At B, circle 10 metres diameter left,' he yells, causing wife Pamela to screech: 'It's 15 metres, you myopic fool!'

The judge raises her eyebrows and deducts two marks for use of voice.

Pam finishes the circle and is looking expectantly at John.

Alas, the letters on the test sheet are starting to blur and he's missed the command to canter.

As Pam skids to a halt instead and begins hollering at her husband, the judge rings the bell for elimination. Five minutes later, she's still ringing it, unnoticed – she'll get tinnitus at this rate, but at least it's drowning out the swearing.

The Ambitious Mum

SUSIE wanted a horse all her life, and buying Rinkydinky two years ago for her daughter Emily was the realisation of a dream… so she'll be damned if she'll let her ungrateful offspring lose interest so soon.

Susie's up at five to ensure Dinks is fed, groomed and out in the field before she takes Emily to school and goes to work.

And because Emily's often so tired by the rigours of juggling homework, her mobile phone and Facebook, Susie has a number of paid riders on hand for those nights when Emily 'just can't face' riding.

Weekends are a whirl of shows and training.

Husband David despairs of ever seeing his wife without wisps of straw stuck to her body-warmer and muck under her once manicured nails.

Friends suggest she should bow to the inevitable and admit that Emily's grown out of ponies, but Susie's not so sure.

Maybe she just needs a more demanding mount and a real goal…

So she's looking for a snazzy 14.2hh and a dressage trainer, while her daughter trawls the net for gap-year projects that will take her as far away from Wiltshire as possible.

The Boxing Day Meet

LILY and Freckle are beside themselves. Usually taken only to quiet meets where Mummy is close at hand, this year they are allowed to attend the Boxing Day meet.

Many a hardened hunting man baulks at the prospect. Nothing during the season is more likely to bring distress to anyone sitting on anything more fiery than a 26-year-old riding school hack – and even they have been known to get flighty.

It is a dangerous combination of hangovers, hoards of well-wishers and a horse who has spent the festive season cooped up in the stable – it's too dreary to wash your horse on Christmas Day and Granny's flamethrower cocktails put paid to any activity after 1pm.

Everyone knows that Boxing Day is when the hunts show the public what a cherished part of the tradition they are and so all know that best behaviour is the only thing acceptable today. This, if anything, adds to the atmosphere of mild panic.

Amid the confusion, Lily is ecstatic. She's eaten three mince pies and been given a nip of something tasty. Freckle is patted and feted by well-wishers who are more than a little terrified of the other snorting beasts backing into each other and their red-faced riders. As the rest of the field set off at a sideways trot, Freckle sedately brings up the rear to a round of applause and festive cheers.

The Beleaguered Husband

WHILE Penelope enjoys a G&T on the sofa, fingering today's bouquet of rosettes, Ian struggles to reverse the lorry into the yard before mucking it out. Weekdays, he may be CEO of his own firm, but somehow the most menial jobs always fall to him at the weekend. The curvaceous creature he fell for in jacket and jods 15 years ago has turned him into a saddle-hefting, fly-spraying drone.

Flushed with success, Penelope sent home early the groom she'd hired for the day (with a joint account cheque), pressing a crisp £20 tip (from Ian's wallet) into her hand as she left. Then Penelope vanished, too, to feed Sophocles' Sorcerer (aka Scoffer) Polos and praise while he 'thaws out' under the solarium.

Ian, she assumes, will not need to thaw out, since he's got fully-breathable, neoprene lined, storm-sealed everything for damp days like these – there's always a theme to Penelope's birthday presents. 'Things you'll need when you're at shows with me' covers it, pretty much. But Ian would trade them all, just for leave to stay at home and watch the Ryder Cup.

The Conditional Jockey

DECLAN models himself on Ruby Walsh. He watches endless videos of his races, practising finishes on the sofa arm. He's seriously thinking of dying his hair grey, to get that 'silver fox' look, and self-consciously talks like his hero – very fast in an impenetrable Co Carlow accent – despite the fact that Declan grew up on the outskirts of Slough.

Declan landed his job with trainer Valentine fforbes-fforbes because his old man rode a Hennessy winner for Val's father 20 years ago. Aged 18, Declan rode 15 point-to-point winners in his first season, but is never allowed to get above himself – the Guv'nor has a handy way with a bucket of cold water if he ever oversleeps or lets a horse get out.

Besides the odd soaking, life is looking up for Declan. He rode his first televised winner last weekend, and the stable lass he followed up the gallops first lot actually smiled at him. Unless it was just a bit of Fibresand in her eye…

Hunt Secretary

VIRGINIA is the chancellor, treasurer, attorney general and front-of-house at the Old Siddlbury hunt, never mind just 'hon sec'. She has huge, jangling pockets and a memory for people that would serve Interpol brilliantly, if it could but harness it. She locks unfamiliar faces with a wide, fixed grin while she mentally works out who they are, if she knew they were coming and what they should be paying. They know they've passed muster when, relieved of 60 quid, a hot port and sausage roll wings its way towards them.

Without her, the hunt would have folded half a century ago, but thanks to Ginny's industry the OSH's coffers are nicely in the black.

With caps collected, anyone who looks to be enjoying the stirrup cup too much will be asked about hunt ball tickets, hound sponsorship or Supporter-Club fees, on a never-ending fund-raising whirlygig.

Ginny's horse, Jonny, is 25 but still going strong. He thrives on boiled barley each Saturday evening, and the knowledge that he has a very responsible job as the hon sec's conveyance. Ginny, who has neither a mobile phone nor computer, has no doubt about the secret to her efficiency: 'A notebook by the phone and a well trained husband.'

The Trainer's Hack

LIKE many middle-aged males, Roving Charmer's girth may be rather more expansive than in days past, but he remains a fine sporting specimen and irresistible to the fillies – in his eyes, if no one else's.

The truth is that Rover was one of racing's nearly-men – plugging away valiantly but never taking the top prize.

However, his willingness to hump hefty weights around handicaps secured his role as trainer's hack to a governor streaking ahead in the expanding waistline stakes and who favours what could be described kindly as a traditional hunting seat at all times.

But Rover doesn't grumble about hauling the boss up the hill. Once there he's in prime position to eye up the gals as they gallop past. For the most part he stands frozen to the spot, throwing in the odd foot stamp or sideways dance to remind all present that these wannabes would be left in his wake.

In fact, Rover's mightily relieved that the governor favours nothing more energetic than a sedate, if not unsteady, canter. Once back home the real work starts – charming the most important lady in his life. Rover's lass showers him with praise and Polos and would be his perfect woman if only she'd stop referring to him as 'old boy'.

The Holidaying Hunter

IT'S only been a few weeks since the last meet of the season, but already Herbert the hunter is looking distinctly rotund, not to mention rather less glossy.

Turned out in his paddock, he spent the first hour or so kicking up his heels, but once the novelty of that – he would never, ever, bolt in the hunting field – has worn off, he is content to graze and, perhaps, relive in his mind the red-letter days of the season.

As a hunter hireling, Herbert is much in demand – for his manners, his respect for hounds, his fifth leg and his good looks – and he has done 30 days between November and March.

Those good looks are not so much in evidence now, though; he's getting a little whiskery and slightly unkempt. The first thing he

did this morning when he was turned out was to canter down to the stream, where he knows the ground is always deliciously squishy, and had a jolly good roll. When he comes in tonight he'll need a thorough grooming, but 'his girl' never complains – Herbert's her favourite too, as he is everyone else's.

Until then, he can graze and daydream, and it won't be too long before the end of the summer, when he'll be fittened up ready for the new season. Herbert can't wait…

The Village Fête Pony

THE village fête is Plum's favourite day of the year. This portly pensioner sees himself as the original galloping gourmet, so making umpteen trips up and down the edge of the village green, carrying squealing children flapping the reins like extras from Bonanza, is a small price to pay for an afternoon where the titbits are on tap. Not only is there an endless supply of Polos, but toffee apples, custard creams, scones and even the odd slurp of beer are proffered.

Of course, there's always a couple of smarty-pants kids who think they can ride. Year after year they attempt to get Plum on the bit and boot him into an indigestion-inducing trot. Putting in a few energetic strides and then pulling his head down suddenly to graze usually sorts them out, while keeping Plum entertained throughout the afternoon.

Disaster nearly struck last year though when, despite his owner's best efforts, the girth would not reach around Plum's barrel-like tummy. Thankfully, an elasticised version was found and now the only downer on this day of feasting and mischief is that it means an annual wash and brush up. But every cloud has a silver lining, so even having his unruly mane pulled at least ensures Plum can get a better look at the treats while waiting in the queue.

The Equestrian Journalist

IT'S the coldest day of the year so far, and while Irene's body is in an indoor arena in Berkshire, her mind is languishing on a deserted beach in St Lucia.

Unfortunately, there isn't enough equestrian action going on in the Caribbean to merit a move there, so she's stuck with the Home Counties for now.

Spotting a certain competitor lurking near the scoreboards, Irene pulls her woolly hat lower over her eyes and shrinks into her oversized Puffa. The last time she'd interviewed that rider, she'd written a glowing account of her win in the novice 24 test at Little Piddleton Manor, only to receive a phone call the minute the report came out, berating Irene at length for not putting her horse's photograph on the cover. This is one of her occupational hazards, along with riders who will only answer 'yes, I'm really pleased' to every question she puts to them.

To be fair, 95% of the time, Irene adores her job – spending day after day at different competitions, going to stately homes for three-day events, sitting at county shows in the sunshine (occasionally), and meeting all those jubilant riders, from the little kid who's just won a lead-rein class to the famous show jumper who's just picked up a cheque for more than Irene earns in a year.

And for all the days she reports at tiny little shows, shivering on the sidelines, there are those big, glamorous competitions with the hi-tech press rooms, endless supplies of coffee and biscuits and top-class action to comment upon.

Shame about some of the other equestrian journalists there, who turn up to four shows a year, name-drop loudly and bag all the best seats in the media section. Still, you can't have it all – and when it comes down to it, Irene wouldn't dream of doing any other job.

The Hunt Ball Organiser

POLLY is starting to panic. What had seemed like a more than fabulous idea at the time has suddenly taken on nightmarish proportions. Granted, the decision to accept the mantle of hunt ball organiser – more like a poisoned chalice in hindsight – was taken on the hunting field, blood up, hip flask fuelled, bright eyed and bushy tailed. Not for her the cynicism of the old guard who melted away muttering platitudes when the subject arose. What could be more fun than setting the shire alight?

Clasping a calming post-hunting drink, Polly realises that the muttered promises and hand-clasping generosity that greeted her appointment were a mere smokescreen. The dreaded auction – the fund-raising behemoth of the season – still only contains a couple of donated turkeys and a variety of coloured brushing boots.

The sudden look of preoccupation that graced the faces of the field that morning has started to make her feel like a leper and, to top it all off, she has just received a call from Muddles Marquees to tell her the tent has started to flood.

How she went from belle of the ball to gibbering wreck she still doesn't know, and it is starting to dawn on her that the thrill of bagging a table next to the dance floor is perhaps not compensation enough. As the phone starts ringing yet again, Polly braces herself for the onslaught of demanding partygoers and grumbling volunteers and wishes more than anything that she was one of them.

The Frosty Fence Judge

'*STAND* back PLEASE! Horse approaching.'

It's Jane's first season's fence judging, and she hasn't felt this powerful since she was on jury service.

But, honestly, these riders who keep trying to clamber all over her fence… don't they realise the competition has started?

She's a good mind to chase them off with her flags, but earlier attempts to do that resulted in a stampede from a rather irritable vet, doctor and fence-builder.

After six hours at her post, and two thermoses of tea, Jane is dying for a pee, but is blowed if she's handing over her clipboard to her assistant even for a minute.

She resolves to hold out to the end, but the effort makes her crotchety: 'I'm sorry – outside assistance! I shall have to notify the steward,' she hollers after an excited mum cries: 'Kick on, darling!'

Delivering her lunch tray, the senior fence judge makes a mental note to put Jane on the lane crossing next year.

The Reluctant Fashionista

THE day of reckoning has arrived. At the grand old age of 10, Gerald is feeling the cold a bit. Although his creamy coat has seen him through many a snappy Gloucestershire winter, Gerald is loathe to admit that he may, after all, be in need of one of those ghastly dog coats.

For years now he has cocked a snook at the world of doggy fashion and many a horse trial has been spent trotting past those stalls that sell canine clothing.

To make matters worse Audrey, his beloved owner, has just popped another sprog. This means two things for Gerald. First, Audrey, whom he adores with an ardent canine passion, will be focusing all her attention on this strange noisy creature. Second, those bracing walks really have gone out the window. Mind you, if the coat is going to become de rigueur, perhaps avoiding ritual

humiliation in the village won't be such a bad thing.

But he will miss those chilly outings and even those two grumpy Friesians who seem to get far too much pleasure out of chasing him.

Drowning in self-pity, Gerald doesn't notice his mistress entering the room.

'Come along, darling,' she beams, 'we're going cow-spotting – I've finally given in and hired a nanny. And just look at this sweet little jacket I've bought you.'

Gerald needn't have worried. The unwritten rules of Gloucestershire still prevail – dogs over humans. Even if the odd sacrifice needs to be made.

The Hunting Heavyweight

CAMILLA has been hunting since before she was born.

'Good old Mama hunted non-stop. Had just cleared a nasty blackthorn with a ditch either side when she got the first twinges. Three hours later I popped out,' she booms at Tilly. Tilly is awed into silence. She has never met anyone like Camilla – few people have.

A newcomer to the hunting field, Tilly is Camilla's favourite prey. The old guard – although no one is smart enough or well-mounted enough for her exacting standards – have long learnt to feign deafness or retreat in the wake of her acid tongue. There is a rumour she once sent a master home, and there have been enough mortified pretenders skewered by her merciless barbs that the rest are running scared.

But Tilly thinks she's a hoot. And Camilla knows a genuine hunting spirit when she sees it. Tilly is immersed in the hunting tales of old and midway through the season is as intolerant as Camilla of incorrect attire and slapdash manners. The handing out of hunt buttons willy-nilly induces a joint apoplexy.

None of the hunt regulars can understand why the old dragon has bestowed the nod of approval on Tilly, but Camilla feels at ease – she has found someone, at last, to whom she can hand over her reins.

And she has made sure that they will be made in her image.

The Jekyll and Hyde Show Pony

WILMINGTON Gloriously Beautiful Lady is a picture – a bright bay with black points (and only the tiniest touch of boot polish). She stands four-square and looks demurely at the judge from under impossibly long lashes. Her quartermarks are immaculate, her plaits pure perfection and her coat glistens (with only the tiniest touch of baby oil).

The other 138cm competitors assume they haven't a chance and glower at Lady's pretty rider, Imogen-Jayne, who is also impossibly smart. Imogen-Jayne and Lady are pulled in top of the line after the initial go-round – the pony does have a lovely walk and no one has a hope of toppling them. Or so you'd think. If only they could see the glint in Lady's eyes, then they might be tempted

to place a bet because, when she is called out for her individual show, Lady has a few extra gaits to impress the judges – not to mention an array of 'airs above the ground'. She starts off serenely enough, but when asked to trot she runs crabwise before unleashing a volley of startlingly athletic bucks down the far side. She tops it off by rearing at the halt, almost unseating Imogen-Jayne, who has stuck like a limpet thus far.

Back in line, Lady stands perfectly. Butter wouldn't melt…

The C-list Rider

CHANELLE is tired of being dismissed as a MAW (model, actress, whatever). Her column inches are dwindling, and having tried and failed to kick-start a pop career, she decides to try a different route and buys a Lusitano dressage stallion instead. If *Wow!* magazine doesn't want her on the cover anymore, then maybe *H&H* will.

Oscar Deala Rental is providing the perfect escape from the pressures of fame. His long mane goes perfectly with Chanelle's chestnut hair extensions, and she's already commissioned a Madonna-esque painting of her and Oscar looking lovingly into each other's eyes. There are a few downsides to her new-found passion, however. She's finding it unbearably painful doing sitting trot – there isn't a sports bra in existence that can cope with that amount of silicone.

And now Oscar has developed an illogical fear of Chanelle's beloved Chihuahua, and is refusing to leave the stable when he's around.

Despite that, following Chanelle's first victory at unaffiliated prelim level, her PR is spreading word of possible British team selection, and offering exclusive interviews to every magazine in the country.

The Reluctant Loader

BRAVURA Boy has tried very hard to overcome his fear.

'Phobia, from the Greek word phobos – it's just an irrational thought process,' says Humphrey, the yard hack and resident smart Alec. 'Think rationally and you'll be fine.'

For the umpteenth time, Bravura Boy rues the day he was given the box next to Humphrey. How could someone whose one racecourse appearance was a three-mile slog round Cartmel, understand the terror of the stalls?

Bravura Boy has never been a fan of confined spaces – not that he's claustrophobic, of course. He had only just conquered his dread of the lorry when he was introduced to the horror of the stalls. Why did Dad have to be so brilliant over 5f? Was there any chance he could make it in the stalls-free world of National Hunt?

But that speedy gene failed to skip a generation so every raceday turns into an epic, and undignified, battle between horse and handler. In his younger days, Bravura Boy had been caught out by their sneaky methods – a pick of grass here, walking in a jolly circle there – but he has wised up over the years.

Sadly, Dad also passed down his desperate-to-please gene,

meaning that Bravura Boy would never dream of actually missing a race. Sliding into the stalls, much like a cork being squeezed back into a bottle, he consoles himself with the fact that, while it may take the strength, determination and patience of six men to shoehorn him into those bloody stalls, there's no thoroughbred in the land who leaves them quicker.

The Short-Straw Vet

IT'S Christmas Eve and Joe is in a stable, reassuring the young creature before him as another fierce contraction grips her body. An inquisitive sheep looks on from next door.

Joe guessed this would happen. Get lumbered with the Christmas on-call shift and some quadruped, somewhere, is bound to have a troublesome labour.

It's a first foal for this five-year-old Welsh Cob-cross, and while she groans her way to the production of a colt, her owner is having kittens.

'I didn't realise it would take this long. Is this normal, Mr Smith? Should she be making that noise?'

Such is her anxiety that it takes several heavy hints before a cup of tea and a mince pie are produced.

'Thank you, Mrs Jones. Just what the vet ordered!'

After a bit of subtle manipulation, a handsome colt finally tumbles into the straw.

'Jesus!' exclaims Joe, oblivious to the irony. 'He's a big 'un. Well done girl, no wonder you were struggling.'

Joe pats the damp neck of the mare.

'What's she called, anyway?' he asks her owner, belatedly.

'You won't believe me if I tell you,' replies Mrs Jones. 'Mary, of course.'

The Snack-Stop Pony

WALLACE rubs his hooves in glee. After a tough winter, his jockey has finally got the measure of him and his 'snacking' sibling number four is now perched precariously on his back, legs not reaching below the saddle, and washing-line reins blowing in the wind. Unfortunately for Wallace, Mother is on the end of the lead-rein helping little Harry get the hang of things, and the rather unsightly baler twine seems to be keeping his head up.

But, however hard he tries to think saintly thoughts, Wallace just can't take his mind off food – it's simply too tempting when there's spring grass all around that seems to be screaming, 'Eat me, eat me!' What an outrage to walk all over it without stopping to sample a little something, he thinks.

Finally the opportunity comes. Mother lets go of the rope to open a gate and, moving quicker than he has done for a while, Wallace seizes the moment. He takes the plunge, snapping the baler twine grass-reins clean in half, and catapulting little Harry clean over his head. Ignoring the wailing infant, Wallace tucks in. As he lifts his head, green grass stuffed in every corner of his mouth, life seems pretty good again.

The Seasoned Hunter

BORIS has done 40 days a season for 10 years, without taking a lame step.

Hauled out of a bog in Ireland and lunged over some cavernous drains and banks in the Limerick country, he was so delighted by the smooth green turf and neat little hedges on his first day in England that he hasn't put a foot wrong since, just in case he's sent back.

His owner, the Colonel, isn't so steady on his pins these days and has a tendency to nod off during checks (particularly if the hipflask has dropped below the halfway mark),but it's Boris's mission in life to return him home to Mrs Colonel in the state he left her.

Approaching a big set of rails, Boris gently shakes the reins out of his master's hands and finds his own stride. He really doesn't think the Colonel is going to be of much help at this stage. And on landing Boris often has to shift a bit to the left or right to catch the old man, who might not come down quite where you'd expect.

Occasionally he gets a day with the Colonel's teenage granddaughter, and gets a rush of blood to the head, squealing and bucking across the first field. But he always looks frightfully apologetic afterwards.

The Hunt Ride Honey

CLARE can no longer drive past a hedge without looking out for the spot where she would jump. In fact, there are few gates or natural objects that don't have that affect on her at the moment. The trip to the stables has become something of a nightmare, especially as the tension mounts for the Pork Pie Classic.

The infamous hunt ride takes place over exquisite country. Proper old-style hedges beckon the unwary to take them on, and somewhat dangerously the entries are open to anyone who wants to have a go.

The thought of last year, when she was beaten to the post by David the heavyweight farmer riding a part-bred shire, still infuriates Clare. How he did it is anyone's guess, but this year is going to be different.

Three fourths, a couple of near misses and a whiff at the top spot have combined to make Clare determined that winning the coveted golden pie is her right by now.

The big day arrives and horse and rider are in fine fettle. Every competitive inch is squeezed out, and her jodhpurs squeezed on. There's always the chance that the chap who has his eye on her might not have his eye on the fence.

Coming to the last, the plan appears to have worked, as the dratted David – this year slimmed down and riding a Thoroughbred – looms up alongside. A strategic wiggle and he ends up in the hedge (he will never admit to anyone exactly why) and Clare soars over to clinch the coveted prize.

The HOYS First-Timer

THE noise is unbelievable. Shouts and whoops from the crowd, a background buzz from the trade stands and the bars, the burble – audible even in the collecting ring – of the commentators and the enthusiastic music from the band, the base note of which seems to be a constant 'boom, boom, boom'.

Oh no, Sally realises, that's her knees knocking.

But Wilson, bless him, looks super. His black bits gleam and his white bits glow, his tack is immaculate and his eyes – although she can't seem them behind all that hair – are bright with interest and excitement.

Since they qualified back in July, Sally has been longing for this moment. She was lucky enough to visit Horse of the Year Show once as a treat when she was a child and always, but always, watched it on the TV. But in her wildest dreams she never thought she'd actually be here, herself, about to ride into that hallowed arena.

It's thanks to this chunky, hairy, laid-back and altogether fantastic fellow she bought off the side of a road in Cornwall for £400. He was only supposed to be a fun horse; something to play around with during the weekends to relax from her tedious office job. And now look – here they are at Birmingham.

'Come on, Wilson,' she whispers into his hairy ear as she swings herself up into the saddle, 'you can do it.'